An inquiry into the cause of the increase of pauperism and poor rates; with a remedy for the same, and a proposition for equalizing the rates throughout England and Wales

William Clarkson

BIBLIOLIFE

AN

INQUIRY

INTO

THE CAUSE OF THE INCREASE

OF

PAUPERISM AND POOR RATES;

WITH

A REMEDY FOR THE SAME,

AND

A Proposition for Equalizing the Rates throughout England and Wales.

BY

WM. CLARKSON, ESQ.

LONDON:

Printed by C. Baldwin, New Bridge-street;

AND SOLD BY BALDWIN, CRADOCK, AND JOY, 47, PATERNOSTER-ROW ; J. HATCHARD, PICCADILLY ; AND L. B. SEELEY, 169, FLEET-STREET.

1815.

THE PUBLIC IN GENERAL;

BUT TO

THE HEADS OF PARISHES,

AND

MEMBERS OF THE HOUSE OF COMMONS,

IN PARTICULAR.

THE Author of the following small treatise for ameliorating the condition of the poor, and giving relief to the contributors in general, but more particularly to those who are the least able to bear so heavy a burden as the collection for the maintenance of the poor, which has been yearly increasing, has for some years past considered it practicable to give proper assistance to the really impotent, aged, and infirm, and check that desire for receiving parish relief which exists at present, but which in former times was considered degrading, and attached a kind of slur on those who applied for it : and he has for more than three years past endeavoured to procure the best information, and put on paper such ideas as occurred to him as the most likely to obtain the great object referred to ; but observing at various times notices being given in the House of Commons by Members thereof, that propositions would be brought forward regarding the Poor Laws, he withheld from the public his ideas on the subject under the expectation that something efficacious would be put into practice ; but in this he has been disappointed.

The delay, however, has been the means of his seeing confirmed his opinion of common beggars, and the absurdity of giving relief indiscriminately, by evidence before a Committee of the House of Commons.

The principle of his plan he has communicated to a few, whose situation in life was likely to make them judges of the practicability and efficacy of it, and through whose desire and recommendation he now presumes to lay it before the Public, under an expectation that it may meet with the concurrence of some Gentleman in the Legislature who may have the ability and inclination to bring it forward in the House of Commons.

Any proposition to make mankind virtuous, and consequently happy, by doing away corruptions which may exist in the Church Establishment, will probably be like kicking against the pricks. Self-interest is so predominant a passion, that to get the master of and subdue it requires much fortitude and resolution : however, every attempt that is made may do something towards stopping the gangrene before the whole body is destroyed ; and it should be recollected that a voluntary abandonment of an evil would be much more creditable, and attended with less loss and inconvenience to the possessors of preferment than a compulsory one : the latter has taken place a few years ago close to our doors, and the consequences of it, it is well known, have brought ruin and destruction on those concerned : it will be well, therefore, for those who are interested to keep it from entering their dwellings.

Notwithstanding this evil may not be immediately removed, or the other part of the Author's plan and regulations put generally into practice by an Act of Parliament, yet he presumes to think that if such part as is practicable was adopted, by parishes adjoining each other coalescing in the maintenance of their poor, and by giving profitable employment to those who apply for relief, and are able to work, the rates might be much reduced, the aged and infirm be made more comfortable, and both rich and poor benefited by the arrangement.

Under the idea that it will in some way or other prove beneficial to the country, the Author recommends it to the impartial perusal and consideration of the community; at the same time soliciting the forbearance of the critic regarding the diction, as plain language, accompanied with truth and common sense, are more his province and desire than any attempt to produce a literary composition.

November, 1815.

INQUIRY

THE INCREASE OF PAUPERISM.

IT has been represented by some, that providing for the poor by enacted laws is an evil,
and a preventative to the general industry
and welfare of the community. But however
respectable the authors of such reasoning may
be, I cannot advocate it, nor consider it consistent either with the laws of God or nature;
neither of which will, in my opinion, justify
such a doctrine; because it appears evident
both from the one and the other that we
ought to assist our distressed fellow creatures,
and particularly such as through natural infirmities, unforeseen misfortunes, or old age,
are rendered incapable of providing for
themselves the necessary food and raiment,
during their existence in this world. The
care of the poor ought, therefore, to be a
great legal object; for without compulsion on
the opulent it is to be feared that many would
experience a greater degree of want and

misery than they do under the present existing laws: besides, giving relief to our really
distressed fellow creatures is conformable to
the Christian religion, and shows the excel-
lency of it; for before its introduction no
public charities were known. That great
impositions are practised for want of proper
management and attention in the fulfilment
of the laws there cannot be any doubt: and
it is to be presumed that great improvements
may be made in the mode of employing the
poor; for that many capable of work are
maintained without it is certain; and that
there is an inequality in the charge to those
who ought to contribute in a proportionate
degree, is also a fact which cannot be
doubted. That a difference should be made
between the really distressed object and the
lazy profligate, must also appear reasonable;
because by giving to each equal relief, a great
evil will naturally arise, inasmuch as it acts
as an encouragement to others to follow the
example of the latter, which must have a
tendency not only to increase the rates, but
also to encourage vice, idleness, and extra-
vagance.

If evils, therefore, do exist, which cannot,
I presume, be doubted, it behoves every
person who has thought at all upon the sub-

ject, and to whom any idea of improvement may occur in economising the vast sums paid, to make the same known. Most persons are capable of adding something to the common stock; and no one's contribution should be rejected, if it appears to be thrown in with a view of benefiting the community; for in a multitude of counsellors there must be some wisdom. No individual, therefore, should be discouraged from making his ideas known, because it is probable they may not prove quite efficacious; for is one shower of rain in the year sufficient to moisten and fertilize the land, or one gleam of the sun's rays to ripen the corn and fruits of the earth, or to exhale the over damps and vapours which are deposited in the same period of time? It has been said, and, it must be allowed, with truth, that whatever a person does with a good intent ought to be looked upon with a charitable eye; for intentions are at least the seed of good actions, and every man ought to sow them, and leave it to the soil and the seasons whether they come up or no, and whether he or any other gather the fruit. An eminent writer has also observed, " that whoever applies himself to collect observations upon the state and operation of the Poor Laws, and to contrive remedies for their imperfec-

tions and abuses, and communicates his ideas
to those who are likely to carry them into
effect, deserves well of a class of the community, so numerous that their happiness makes
no inconsiderable part of the whole." It is
true, in all new institutions or regulations
difficulties may at first arise, it being no easy
matter to lay a perfect foundation at once;
but that ought not to discourage perseverance; for the arts of life advance but gra-
dually, every thing being progressive and few
things brought to perfection at once, but most
may by wisdom and perseverance attain it in
time; for as Dr. Johnson observed, " All the
performances of human art at which we look
with praise or wonder, are instances of the
resistless force of perseverance; it is by this
the quarry becomes a pyramid, and that
distant countries are united by canals; small
operations, incessantly continued, in time
surmount the greatest difficulties; mountains
are levelled, and oceans bounded, by the
slender force of human beings." Those,
therefore, who wish to gain any particular
object, should add to their reason and spirit
the power of persisting in their purposes.
Embracing this idea, I shall endeavour to
give what has suggested to me to be both
efficacious and practicable; and although I

may not reap much advantage should the harvest prove propitious, it is my sincere wish that others may. On entering upon a work of such consequence and magnitude, it appears to be essentially necessary to ascertain where the defect in the present system lies, and then apply a remedy, as a skilful physician would do in making an attempt to cure a disease of the human body.

It would seem then that the defect, according to the opinion of some, must arise, first, from a deficiency of employment for the labouring poor, arising from an augmentation of population to a greater degree than the sources of employment; secondly, wages inadequate to the price of provisions; thirdly, a corruption of morals, and the consequent loss of that spirit of independence which formerly possessed the hearts of the labouring poor; or, fourthly, bad laws, or bad management of the laws.

To me the first does not appear to be the cause of the evil under consideration, because the population of the country has by no means kept pace with the augmentation of the rates, as I shall show by giving a statement derived from returns made to Parliament for five specified years.

Year.	Population, about	Amount of Rates.	Amount according to the increased Population.	Difference more.
		£	£	£
1688	5,300,000	665,362		
1776	7,728,000	1,530,804	970,173	560,631
1783 } 1785 }	8,016,000	2,004,238	1,006,328	997,910
1792	8,675,000	2,645,520	1,089,059	1,555,461
1803	9,168,000	4,267,965	1,150,950	3,117,015

Having shown by this table that the rates
have increased considerably beyond the proportionate increased population, being in the
last specified year nearly treble, it is but
reasonable to state that it does not altogether
arise from the increased number of poor; for
the difference in the value of money has naturally operated to enhance the amount, at the
same time the effect of the extra burthen on
those who have had no means of increasing
their income in the same period must be
severely felt, let the cause be what it may.

It may further be proper to remark on
reasonable presumption, that there is no
deficiency of employment, the resources from
which having annually increased with the
wealth of the country, which naturally increases the demand for labour; besides, there
are about one hundred and fifty different modes

of employment for males and females already, as particularised by Mr. Colquhoun; and taking into consideration the increasing demand for many manufactures that we cannot fully supply, for we import sail-cloth, canvas, and linen, cordage, tow, and yarn, it is clear that these as well as other branches may be increased both for home consumption and also for the supply of our colonies. From such sources of productive labour there ought not to be an individual in the vigour of life and free from sickness, whose industry should not contribute to the means of subsistence ; for a want of work but seldom occurs : on the contrary does it not often happen that master workmen are obliged to be slaves to their men through a dread of their departure? also farmers in busy times for want of labourers? nay, do not we see recruiting serjeants in the time of war offering large bounties for men, and unable to get them? Are not all these testimonies that work is generally to be had when there is a desire to obtain it? Besides, admitting there is already a deficiency, it should be recollected that a great part of England, Scotland, and Ireland, remain uncultivated, which would afford a further source of employment for our increased population. The partial complaints we may hear

of the want of work arises in a general way
from those who use it as a cloak for idleness,
and not from any real deficiency of work ;—
it is true, in large societies there will always
be some bad subjects whom the laws, however
perfect they may be, cannot restrain ; at the
same time the utmost ought to be done that
is practicable to make mankind diligent, virtuous, and happy.

I shall, in addition to the before-mentioned
table, now give a comparative statement of
the actual number of paupers in the years
there mentioned, and the number according
to the increased population, that it may be
seen in what proportion they have diminished
or increased.

Year.	Population of England and Wales, about	Number of Paupers relieved.	Number of paupers in proportion to population.	Difference in number according to the population.	
1688	5,300,000	563,964			
1776	7,728,000	695,177	822,323	127,146	less than the proportion.
1785	8,016,000	818,851	852,968	34,117	
1792	8,675,000	955,326	923,092	32,234	more than the proportion.
1801	8,872,980	No Return	944,158		
1803	9,168,000	1,040,716	975,551	65,165	

In addition to the last number of paupers,
there were 194,052 vagrants relieved in 1803

at an expence of 19,405*l.* 4*s.* making the whole number 1,234,768.

By the foregoing table it appears, that in 1776 and 1785, the actual number of paupers were not equal to the increased population, but in more recent years, viz. 1792 and 1803, the number which received relief exceeded considerably the proportion of population; which shows most unquestionably a great defect of late, which will in all probability increase if the system is not changed or some improvement made.

I shall, secondly, give a statement of the price of bread, average money wages of husbandry, and the bread wages, in each of the said periods, also for the years 1811 and 1812, with a view of showing that the wages have by no means kept pace with the price of that necessary article.

Year.	Price of bread per quartern.	Money wages of husbandry.	Bread wages in quartern loaves.
	d.	s.	
1688	3	6	24
1776	6½	8	15
1785	6	8	16
1792	7	9	15
1803	10	10	12
1811	12	12	12
1812	20	15	9

In the last year I have over-rated the aver-

age price of wages, for in Wiltshire, Devon-
shire, and Cornwall, wages are considerably
lower than in other counties in England, and
have seldom, I understand, exceeded nine
shillings a week ; it may therefore be presumed the average has not exceeded twelve
shillings. It appears from this, that the
price of husbandry wages has by no means
kept pace with the price of provisions, taking
bread as the criterion, and it being by far the
principal article of food for the labouring
class, and particularly where there are children, it is, therefore, a proper standard by
which a suitable judgment may be formed.
In further confirmation of the foregoing, it
appears also from returns made, that the
paupers in agricultural counties exceed those
in manufacturing, and that the rates in Dorsetshire are nearly double those in Cumberland,
although there is not much difference in
the population, the former being 115,319,
and the average rates in 1803, 4s. $2\frac{1}{4}d.$ per £.
whilst the population of the latter was 117,230,
and the rates only 2s. 8d. per £.; the amount
raised in Dorsetshire being 78,358l. and in
Cumberland, only 34,896l.; this, however,
may arise from the more frugal habits of the
labouring people in Cumberland, or from
their superior knowledge in the culinary art ;

in either case they are worthy of imitation. The industry of the husbandmen (who are one-third of the whole population) being of more importance than any other to the existence of the people at large, (for without the raising of food no society could exist) it is therefore highly proper they should receive wages adequate to their labour and maintenance, so as to make them independent of charitable assistance, and operate to keep up their number.

In the foregoing statement of the amount of Poor-rates, it will be seen I have only taken in the rates as per return made to Parliament up to the year 1803, being the last return made ; but calculating the number of paupers according to the proportionate increase of population *only* (although, judging from previous years, the increase must be greater) and the price of bread, it will appear that the paupers in 1811 would amount to 1,189,131, exclusive of vagrants; the population of England and Wales being 10,488,000, and the rates for the poor, exclusive of county rates, &c. would amount to 4,882,461*l.*; and in the year 1812, the paupers would amount to 1,208,125, the population being about 10,653,000, and the rates as before-mentioned would be 8,265,453*l.* which sum I have no doubt will prove rather under than over the actual amount.

However, taking it at that sum only, viz.............£8,265,453
And add to it the annual produce of lands and money be-
   queathed at sundry times for the poor, which by
   returns to Parliament in 1785 amounted to 258,701*l.*
   which sum was in all probability short of the real sum;
   and lands, it is well known, have since that period
   advanced considerably; the whole, therefore, with
   bequests made since, may now be called at least   450,000
Add also private benevolence, hospitals and dispensaries
   for the sick, &c. &c. which on a moderate computa-
   tion may be called.   3,284,547

Making a total of.................12,000,000

expended annually for the support of the poor and indigent, which is nearly a fourth part of the present rental of the kingdom; besides which, there have been considerable sums raised for the representatives of deceased, and also for maimed, soldiers and sailors during the war. This evidently shows a defect in the present system of providing for and employing the poor, particularly when it appears by a return made to the House of Commons in 1804, there were only 166,000 of really impotent paupers receiving relief, which was about a seventh part of the number who actually received parish support; and if these 166,000 had been maintained at an expense of three shillings per head per week, the expense would have been 1,294,800*l.* which is little more than a fourth part of what was collected from parishes for the maintenance of the poor, exclusive of private and public charities as already specified. If therefore those who are capable of work were employed, and paid by their respective employers wages equivalent to the price of provisions, which is but just and reasonable, for the labourer is entitled to a suitable remuneration for his work, then certain persons, such as the small stock-holders, annuitants, inferior clergy, officers in the navy and army, inferior tradesmen, &c. &c. would be relieved from an unjust impost, and it would fall equally on all descriptions; for some of the before-mentioned have had no means of increasing their incomes, whilst the rates have increased on them as well as the price of all necessaries of life to a great degree, and the landed proprietors or occupiers have been benefited for the last twenty years beyond any previous time, by the great increase which has taken place in the rents, and also in the production, of the soil ; hence it is incompatible with justice and unreasonable in the extreme to require the first description of persons to assist those who are so capable of bearing the burthen which is so justly their due.

Having then first shown that the rates have increased beyond the proportionate increase of population, and also presumed that there is no deficiency of employment ; and, secondly, made it appear on the most authentic evidence, that inadequate wages have been given ; it becomes necessary, thirdly, to show that the bad state of morals and, the natural consequence, the loss of those highly praise-worthy feelings, the spirit of independence, have increased and operated to enhance the amount of the Poor-rates.

To determine that the present age is an age of degeneracy, it is only necessary to look at the great increase of criminals, which is far beyond the proportion of the extended population; for in 1808 the number of criminals in London were 1,110, out of a population of 909,433, which is in proportion to one in 849; whilst in Scotland there were only 87 out of a population of 1,741,818, which is one in 20,021. What can cause so serious a difference? It may in part arise from the riches and luxury enjoyed by the former in a greater degree than by the latter ; for idleness, want, and misery will increase in proportion to the increase of riches and luxury; but I should be inclined to attribute it in a principal degree to the difference between resident and nonresident clergy and parochial schools, which are and have been prevalent in Scotland, whilst in England there has been a great want of both; for in the year 1793 there were 194,914 children from 5 to 14 years of age permanently relieved in England and Wales by parochial rates, and only 21,600 were in schools of industry receiving but a very indifferent education; so there were 173,000 growing up without any education at all; besides 120,236 under five years old. Since that period a change has happily taken place, which, if persevered in, will, it is to be hoped, have a favourable effect; for it cannot be doubted that education to a certain extent, accompanied with religious instruction and virtuous impressions constantly instilled, will lead the human mind towards useful pursuits, and enable it the more readily, when at a proper age, to form such prudent ideas of a matrimonial connection as are the most likely to enable them to provide for themselves without the assistance of the parish to which they happen to belong.

It may not be improper to remark here, in contravention to a writer of ability on the Poor Laws (Mr. Malthus), but who it may be presumed has committed an error, in considering marriage amongst the lower class of society an evil, because it tends to increase the population; for the decay of population has been thought one of the greatest evils a state can suffer, (particularly where there are so many additional sources of employment,) and the improvement of population is the object which ought to claim the attention of the legislator; besides, the laws of God require "mankind to be fruitful, and multiply, and replenish the earth." Again, " marriage and the bed undefiled, is honourable amongst all men;" and many eminent writers have likewise spoken highly of, and recommended, marriage. Hufeland considered marriage as indispensably necessary for the moral perfection of mankind, for it produces to the state well educated citizens, accustomed from their youth to regularity and an observance of the duties they have to perform ; hence they are most likely to become orderly and useful members of society.

Dr. Paley too says, in substance, that " by marriage, the private comfort of individuals, especially the female sex, is much increased. The greatest number of healthy children are obtained, and the peace of society is increased by preventing contentions in assigning to each man and woman an exclusive right. It also encourages industry; and we have the authority of ancient nations for it. The Spartans and Romans thought it of so much consequence, that the former inflicted penalties on their citizens for not marrying, and the latter encouraged marriage by depriving a man who had no children of one-half of any legacy left him." "The constitution of the sexes is also the foundation for marriage; and should it be prevented, fornication would naturally follow; for all natural passions must be gratified, and fornication (which is prostitution), brings the victims of it almost to certain misery. It also produces habits of ungovernable lewdness, (for irregularities of this kind have no limits), which introduce the more aggravated crimes of seduction, adultery, violation, &c. The criminal commerce of the sexes corrupts and depraves the mind and moral character more than any single species of vice whatsoever: In low life it is usually the first stage in men's progress to the most desperate villanies; it also perpetuates a disease, which may be accounted one of the sorest maladies of human nature, and the effects of it are said to visit the constitution of even distant generations. The Scriptures likewise condemn fornication: ' Out of the heart, ' says our Saviour, ' proceed evil thoughts, murders adulteries, fornication, &c. &c.; these are the things which defile a man;' and St. Paul to the Hebrews says, ' Whoremongers, &c. God will judge."

The great Lord Bacon recommends marriage: he says, " Wives are in youth our mistresses, in middle age our companions, and in old age our nurses:" indeed in participating in each others sorrows, they alleviate the pain, and make misfortune or deprivation the easier to be endured; and as the final view of all rational politics is to produce the greatest quantity of happiness, if matrimony tends to do so, it ought, instead of being checked, to be encouraged; for the happiness of a people is made up of the happiness of individuals, and the quantity of it can only be augmented by increasing the number of the percipients, or the pleasure of their perceptions. At the same time matrimony is recommended, it must be acknowledged that those who are the most ignorant enter into that state in a general way, without the least calculation on the prospect they have of maintaining themselves and their offspring, but are stimulated to it under the expectation of parish relief without work, which consequently makes them less considerate than they otherwise would be; for it is no uncommon circumstance to hear such say, " I don't care, the parish must do for me." It cannot I presume be disputed, that the cultivated mind must be more open to conviction and more capable of eradicating mistaken principles than that which is uncultivated; consequently the present almost general system of giving religious education will in the course of time have, it is to be hoped, a favourable effect.

It is also worthy of observation, that a country flourishes or decays according to the quantum of virtue and industry, or vice and idleness, which exist in the body politic. How necessary, therefore, it is for the higher orders to set a good example; for it is a well established maxim, that the state of morals depends more on the influence of example than on the enforcement of the law: the one conveys lasting conviction, and produces permanent practice; the other, only temporary terror. Virtuous emanations from the head of a nation would, therefore, it is to be presumed, carry reformation and virtue from thence to the lowest orders, in the same manner as from the head of a pure spring we may expect pure water to flow into all the inferior uncontaminated channels; for it is too certain that vicious practices in the higher classes contribute in a great measure to fill

our streets with harlots, our gaols with felons,
and our assemblies with depravity, and also
to that contempt of religion and moral pro-
bity so necessary for the well-being of society:
for it is in vain to look for improvement of
the lower orders, unless the example proceed
from the higher; for whilst the latter remain
corrupt, the former will continue depraved;
and the consequence will be an increase in
the number of paupers, and the evils of
poverty. Another great evil to be mentioned is the practice of our Church Government, as far as regards the mode of appoint-
ing proper men as ministers : for although an
established religion and mode of worship is
no doubt proper, yet it ought to be recollected it is no part of christianity, but only
the means of inculcating it; and religion
being of more consequence to the preservation of a country than its political constitution, and also intended for our well-being in
this world, and our eternal happiness in that
which is to come, it ought to be conducted
on pure principles, free from any mixture of
partiality or self-interest, excepting what
arises from virtue and ability. It ought to
be quite unconnected with Government influence, or influence to Government ; for, to
use the language of an eminent church

divine (Dr. Paley) " every other idea, and every other end, than the preservation and communication of religious knowledge, being mixed with it; as of making of the church an engine, or even an *ally* of the state; converting it into the means of strengthening it as a support of regal, in opposition to popular forms of Government, have served only to debase the institution, and to introduce into it numerous corruptions and abuses." Such persons only, therefore, as have competent abilities, and are of good life, and *really* called by the Spirit of God, as they at present declare to be when ordained, should be appointed to such a sacred office; for as all the members of the body receive spirits from the same head, and are useful and serviceable one to another, thus these brethren receiving the same spirits from their head, Christ, would be more strongly bent to do good one to another; for as the love of God dilates the heart, purifies love, and extends it to all men, it is therefore highly necessary in ministers for the preaching of the gospel, as our Saviour said to St. Peter, " Peter, lovest thou me?" " then feed my lambs." It is absurd to argue, as some persons do, " It matters not what the life of a minister is, provided he gives good advice to his flock;"

for what is the use of superior knowledge, unless it is productive of superior actions? Do not ministers of bad life bring an evil report on God's ordinances, as if no good, no grace, attended them; besides, precept without example is, if I may be allowed the comparison, like mustard without meat, or like meat swallowed down for pleasure or greediness, which only overcharges the stomach, or fumes into the brain; the former, therefore, is in a general way as inefficacious to spiritual nourishment as the latter would be to the body; and it is known that if the stomach takes in more than it is capable of digesting, the superfluity does no good to the body, which it is intended to preserve; and although the ministerial gifts of the preachers of the gospel are for the use of others, yet they ought themselves to lay hold of that salvation they recommend; the same as boxes where perfumes are kept for garments are themselves perfumed by keeping them: for, as Bishop Wilson has said, " The duty of pastors is to convert sinners to God by their *example* as well as by their sermons." We know bad example from equals will debase the human character: how much more, therefore, must it, if it comes from those who by superior education and consequence in life

attract our attention as guides and directors.
The basis of all civil society ought to be laid
in good faith, which cannot subsist without
a conformity of actions with words, without
morals and religion, and without an habitual
reverence of both. " A good name," says the
wise man, " is better than precious oint-
ment; " it is a perfume that recommends the
person it accompanies, that procures him
every where an easy acceptance, and facili-
tates the success of all his enterprises. The
majority of mankind being doomed to the
labour of the body, and not of the mind ; to
lives of action, and not of meditation, they
naturally look up to those as an example for
their conduct whose lot in life is considered
to be of a superior cast. And is it not a further proof of the necessity of good and holy
men to act as ministers, when in our admi-
rable Litany we pray that " bishops, priests,
and deacons, may both by their preaching
and *living* set forth God's holy word, and
that they may evermore serve God in holiness
and pureness of *living*." Besides, have we
not the authority of our Saviour himself for
the necessity of good and faithful ministers,
when he says, " Let your light so shine before men that they may see your *good works*
and glorify your Father which is in heaven."

Again : " Ye are the salt of the earth ; but if the salt have lost its savour, wherewithal shall it be salted ? It is thenceforth good for nothing but to be cast out and trodden under foot of men." It is scarcely necessary to remark, that from this, as well as from our own reason, it appears that the clergy who do not set a good example, and live agreeably to, as well as preach, the gospel, are of no good effect, but should be cast off.

It may be asked, How such excellences are to be met with ? I would answer, As far as it is possible it should be tried for ; and if set about in good earnest it may be accomplished, if not to the utmost extent, in a great degree, from the multiplicity of percipients ; for do we not sow many seeds to procure one superior flower ?

In making these observations, I am not at all apprehensive of giving umbrage to good ministers of the church, of whom there are no doubt many of most exemplary character and conduct ; and should the remarks I have made cause reformation in the licentious and libertine part, or in the future mode of admitting men to so sacred an office, the purpose intended will be accomplished, and we may then look forward with confidence to a diminution of sin, which causeth so large a

portion of human misery, being the forerun-
ner of poverty and disease, which swells the
amount of the rates collected under the name
of Poor Rates. In these remarks, it is not
expected to make all mankind perfect, which
I believe to be morally impracticable ; at the
same time there can be no reason suggested
why they should not be made as good as is
possible; and the way to accomplish so
desirable a thing is to do away bad customs
and introduce good ones. I would, therefore,
that church ministers should be appointed for
their virtue and ability, and have a suitable
and more equitable provision, that their
respectability may be maintained amongst
their respective flocks, and not, as is too often
the case, have a subsistence inferior to common mechanics and small agriculturists, and
in consequence thereof are very often looked
upon by the latter with disdain, instead of respect, whilst others of the same profession are
enjoying, through interest, (without, in many
instances, any regard to ability or inclination
to mend mankind,) their ten thousands a-year
for doing little or nothing, whilst the other
description have little more than their tens,
or at any rate a bare subsistence for much
required duty ; some too partake of a plura-
lity of livings on which it is impossible for
them to reside, do the duty, and set a good

example, however competent they may be for each of these duties; this is an evil of the greatest magnitude and must be corrected before any real benefit can be looked for. It may not be inapplicable to quote the opinion of Bishop Latimer, which, however eccentric it may appear at the present day, must nevertheless be allowed to contain uncontrovertible truths. Speaking of patrons to livings, he says, " They have a great charge and a great burthen before God, if they do not diligently endeavour to place *good* and *godly* men in their benefices, but are slothful and careth not what manner of men they appoint, or else are covetous and will have it themselves, and hire a Sir John Lack-Latin who shall say service, so that the people shall be nothing edified, no doubt such a patron shall make answer before God for not doing his duty." He also speaks of preachers and their keeping residence, by asking and telling who is the most diligent, viz. the devil; he is never out of his diocese, never from his cure, always in his parish, he keepeth residence at all times, he is ready and always at his plough, he causeth patrons to sell their benefices, yea more, he gets himself to the university, and causes great men and esquires to send their sons there, and put out poor scholars, that should be divines; for their parents intend not that they should be preachers, but that they may have a show of learning. Therefore, he says, " ye unpreaching prelates, learn of the devil to be diligent in your office."

It becomes necessary to consider fourthly and lastly, the laws in being, and the management of those laws. The 43d of Queen Elizabeth may be considered a wise and judicious one, for it directs that a sufficient sum shall be raised to purchase a stock of flax, hemp, wood, thread, iron, and other wares and stuff, to set the poor on work ; and also for necessary relief of the lame, impotent, old, blind, and others as are not able to work. The design, therefore, of this law is to give relief *only* to the helpless poor, and employment to such as are able to work; but this it must be known is but partially put into practice, for during near sixty years after the passing of this act it remained stationary, and in the latter period of that time, the general economy of the country was disturbed by civil war, and other troubles of a political nature ; and in later times one would think no such act was in being, as it is now so seldom put into practice. The cause of this may in part arise from the execution of it being placed in hands seldom competent to the task; the interests, habits, and

c

occupations of overseers of the poor so frequently militating against their desire and
ability to perform their duty: for it can
scarcely be disputed that overseers of the
poor, annually elected, and often unwillingly
so, are too short a time in office to acquire a
perfect knowledge of their duty ; independent
of the time and attention their own necessary
avocations require of them, to say nothing of
their unfitness, through want of a proper
knowledge of the undertaking.

There are also many difficulties and vexa-
tions in the law of settlements arising out of
the 13th and 14th Charles II. which have
increased the number of paupers, and furthermore proved a source of litigation as well as
a restraint on the free circulation of labour ;
for if a poor person cannot get work in his
own parish, he is afraid to go to another
where he might find employment ; because,
if unfortunately he becomes distressed through
illness, or any other unforeseen cause, he is
removed at a time, perhaps, when his bodily
infirmities require rest ; or if kept during that
period, the parish to which he belongs must
refund ; but before the parish which has kept
him during sickness can recover, he must be
actually removed, although he may be so far
recovered as to be able to resume his work ;

and when once removed, he must never more return to the parish wherein he had been able to gain a subsistence, on pain of being treated as a rogue and vagabond.

In a manufacturing and commercial country like England, where the demand for labour in different places is continually fluctuating, any law or regulation which may have a tendency of confining a man within his settlement, or to controul him in his desire to carry his industry to any place in the kingdom, appears to me an act of injustice to the labourer as well as an injury to the state, because the individual loses that which he depends on for his support, and may be the cause of his becoming chargeable to the parish; and the public loses the profit on his labour, which diminishes the strength and prosperity of the country, and also increases the amount of the rates. Much expense is also incurred respecting the settlement of wives and children, excepting bastards, who have advantages superior to legitimate children: their settlement is with the father, if known; if not known, with the mother; and if neither are known, then at the place where they are born. But it may be difficult to ascertain any of these points,

c 2

and consequently much litigation and expense is incurred. A woman marrying a second husband, and gaining a new settlement in right of that husband, has been held not to confer the new settlement on her former children, so that a separation between the mother and her children was established by such decision : also, when the father had run away and the mother had resided with a child on an estate of her own, it has been held that neither mother or child could gain a settlement, because they could only derive it from the father. These and other evils attending the law of settlements must be well known, to those who have taken any part in carrying into execution the present laws for the support of the indigent, to occasion the expenditure of large sums in litigation to determine to which parish certain poor persons belong ; so much so, that the law expenses and removals cost in the year 1803 near 200,000*l.* If therefore it is taken into consideration that the number of paupers are very much increased, and the amount of the charge at least double, it will not be unreasonable to calculate the law expenses and removals at this time at 250,000*l.* ; which, with salaries to vestry clerks in more than 14,000 parishes and places, would increase the amount to 350,000*l.* and upwards, the saving of which will hereafter appear practicable.

All paupers born in this country have a right, by the existing laws, to be maintained at the expense of the parish to which they belong; and it is pretty certain they are so maintained in idleness, with the exception of perhaps one in forty or fifty, although there are so many sources of employment, which I have endeavoured to show in answer to the first proposition. Notwithstanding this privilege, it must be allowed that common beggars are very prevalent in this country, although there ought not to be one in it: they think their condition better than that of a pauper, and the impositions and deceptions practised by them are too numerous to mention. Those who are inclined to relieve them should consider, that every penny given is a bounty upon idleness, while every penny spent is a reward to industry; and that that species of humanity is the most injurious which indulges its feelings at the expense of its judgment (if it would only make use of it), and affects a want of power to resist doing a seemingly generous action, although convinced that its ultimate tendency must prove detrimental. Charity, to be consistent with public welfare, should be most solicitous to stop short of encouraging vice, and equally cautious not to injure the principle of industry; for mistaken benevolence weakens the foresight, energy, and bodily exertions in that part of society which are principally composed of the labouring poor, by taking away the necessity of labour. If persons are to be relieved in addition to public institutions, those who afford it should endeavour to select the unfortunate and deserving, and scout and discourage the idle and vicious; as it is proper that such should suffer hardships, both as a punishment and also as a stimulus to drive them into better habits.

In addition to what has already been stated against the existing laws, management, and other things connected therewith, it may be further observed, that there is a very considerable disproportion in levying the rates, both on houses and land, but particularly on the former; for there are houses with appendages annexed in many parts of the country, occupied by the owners, worth 100*l.* a year and upwards, which are not rated in the parish books at more than 20 or 30*l.*; nay, I have heard of some of the value of 100*l.* being rated at only 10*l.* whilst others in the same parish which are rented by persons less able to pay are rated at rack rent.

I have in the former part of this work stated, that if there is now a deficiency of work for the labouring part of the community, which I very much doubt, if we were to put the whole of our means into action, the uncultivated parts of England, Scotland, and Ireland, would afford further employment for our increased population, and that our colonies abroad might also assist us.

I would further remark, that as a large proportion of India is also the property of the people of Great Britain, it is worth while to take into consideration how far it would be proper to send out landholders and labourers for the purpose of cultivating land, &c. in so extensive a country. If such a plan is practicable and consistent, we might reap from its adoption a double advantage ; as in addition to our getting rid of a superfluous population (if such exists), which must impoverish the state, we should add to our wealth by increasing the trade of the country ; for a British population in India would draw from this country our manufactures to a much greater extent than at present ; as the wants of the Hindoos are so limited, the consumption of European goods is extremely small compared to so extensive a country.

Having endeavoured to show in as brief a manner as possible, first, that the increased population does not exceed the sources of employment; and if it did, other means are at hand ; secondly, that inadequate wages have on an average been given for labour ; thirdly, that there exists a corruption of morals beyond former times, and that there is a remedy for the same ; and fourthly, that the laws in being are defective ; that the management is in improper hands; and that there is an inequality of charge on the contributors to the rates; it now becomes necessary I should point out a remedy for the second and fourth proposition ; and in doing so, it will be proper to consider, first, the best and most efficacious plan to be adopted ; secondly, the advantage or benefit to the community attending it; and thirdly, the comfort and melioration of the deserving poor arising therefrom. I must endeavour to show, that the various regulations I am about to propose are likely to embrace these three essential things; in which if I succeed, I shall have gained the object in view; the whole community, both rich and poor, will be benefited by their being put

into practice; and it will be a fit subject
to recommend to the consideration of the
legislature of the country. That plan I apprehend must be the best which, by an *equal*
levying of the rates, and a frugal appropriation
of the sums raised, affords the most comfort
to the object requiring relief; that gives employment to those whose strength will enable
them to partake of it ; that gives equitable
wages to the industrious; and that which has
a tendency to improve the rising generation
in morals and industry. I hope the various
regulations I have to propose, with the adoption of what I have already recommended,
will be considered sufficient to attain all these
points. I shall, agreeable to my proposition,
first take into consideration a remedy for inadequate wages, so as to afford relief to the
industrious husbandman without the necessity
of applying so frequently to magistrates, who
sometimes order it (for want of proper information) when there is no real necessity ; at
the same time it will be proper to consider
the interest of their employers and the community at large, being convinced that, without
a reciprocal advantage, the plan would be bad.
I would therefore propose, that the wages
should be fixed by the magistrates at the
quarter sessions, or four specified times in

the year (i. e. every three months), according to the average price of bread the preceding three months, in the district where the parties reside and labour, allowing three shillings a week in addition to the value of ten quartern loaves, which ten loaves I should consider equivalent to all the food of five in a family, per week; and five to each family of productive labourers is as near the general average as can be calculated according to Mr. Colquhoun's treatise, which is allowing two quartern loaves to each as an equivalent for food; and the extra three shillings as sufficient for clothing, beer, &c.; the further earnings of the wife and children to be appropriated to pay the rent, medical assistance, and for any other reasonable gratification, in addition to the necessary culinary and other work of the house, or to enable them to save a trifle for future exigencies; so that when bread is one shilling per quartern on the average in three preceding months, the wages of the husbandman should be thirteen shillings for the three following months, or any shorter period. It may be said that some have more in family, and some less, which is true; but where there are more, some of the children are in all probability grown up to an age to enable them to add to the stock of their parents; and where the

labourer has a smaller family, or perhaps none
at all, I would in such cases propose, that a
Bank should be formed by the Governor and
Directors of the poor (whom I shall hereafter
mention), who should employ the deposits in
purchasing exchequer bills or other government security, and no other, and who should
not only allow those who place money (the
savings of their industry) therein, four per
cent. per annum, but also a premium in proportion to their wages and yearly savings.
This would act as an excitement to frugality,
and enable those who are in a state of celi-
bacy, when they marry, to commence their
new situation in life with comfort to themselves and advantage to the public; as it
frequently occurs in the present times, that
such persons are unable to procure themselves
a bed to lay down on, or a chair to sit in, and
apply for parish assistance in a short time
after marriage; for if there is in some instances a disposition to save, they know not
in what way to lay it out, and therefore spend
it unnecessarily and improvidently, as is often
the case; which verifies the old saying, that
" the money burns out the bottom of the
pocket."

Having endeavoured to give a short and as
explanatory a method as possible of the
second proposition, I shall proceed in like

manner to the fourth and last, viz. a remedy
for defective laws, bad management, and un-
equal charge to the contributors.

In the first place, in lieu of the present
method of every parish providing for their
own poor, which causeth so much litigation, expense, and inconvenience, as I have
already stated, I would propose to *equalize*
the rates throughout England and Wales,
and make the nation, what it really is, *one
large family;* and that every parish and
place should contribute its proportion to the
general fund according to the *actual* value
of the property it possesses; for as we in-
dividually partake of the general good arising from public institutions, it surely cannot
be considered unreasonable to require an
equal contribution to that which we are benefited by; and that we are all proportionably benefited by the labouring class of
society must appear evident to every thinking
person; as it must be known that the
demand for grown persons from the country
(where the rates are often the highest) to
supply the labour in London and other large
towns, is very considerable; and as these
persons are reared very often wholly or in
part at the parish expense from which they
migrate for the benefit of those towns, it
appears reasonable they should participate in

the expense; for in proportion as any part of
a country or nation is made better, the whole
must be improved, and every individual is
benefited by it. If by equalizing the rates
relief should be given to large manufacturing
towns where the rates are sometimes great, it
will have the tendency of lowering the articles manufactured, and of course enable them
to be sold at a lower rate, and consequently
allow them to be exported at a reduced price,
and so far prevent a competition in foreign
markets; so that any additional sums which
may be paid in local situations will be reimbursed by the cheapness of the articles sold
at a reduced price, besides adding to the
riches and prosperity of the country by an
increased foreign demand, as well as having
the effect of lowering the price of labour; for
in proportion as all or any useful articles are
reduced in price, in the same ratio will the
price of bread, and consequently wages,
experience a reduction.

Again, by equalizing the rates, litigation
would be avoided; because, whether the
person requiring relief belongs to one parish
or another, it would be of little consequence
which should afford the needful assistance,
as the expense would go to the general
fund ; and consequently the enormous sums I
have stated as being expended in litigation

and removals, would be saved ; and it surely must be admitted, that the money would be much better applied in relieving the distressed than spending it in law-suits ; for by the former we are performing one of the christian virtues; whereas by the latter we are encouraging contention and broils, sometimes between neighbours and friends. It was remarked by an eminent Chief Justice, " that armies of counsel were frequently arrayed, to contend about which of two parishes should provide a scanty subsistence to a miserable pauper, with as much zeal as if a title to the first estate in the kingdom were at stake; and at an expense which would probably support fifty such paupers during their lives."

I would also remark, that by congregating a number of persons in one house, (a system I shall hereafter propose) in preference to supporting them in their respective parishes, even were they employed, which is but seldom the case, a considerable saving would naturally arise (independent of the expenses of law suits and removals); for it cannot, I presume, be disputed that a number of persons kept in one habitation may be proportionably maintained at a much less expense than a few, and particularly when a well-digested organized plan is fixed upon for a good, cheap, and nutritious food and clothing, and also suitable employment furnished for such as are able to work; for although the earnings of some may be small, yet little earnings of a large number will amount to something considerable; so will small savings made in various articles consumed by a number of persons; besides which, requiring every person admitted into the house to work, if able, will tend to prevent a number of lazy people from applying for relief who are indifferent about getting their own living; as it is the facility afforded to the idle in procuring relief *without* work that occasions so many applicants, it being customary to apply for a pension of a few shillings a week, which is spent in laziness and rags, without any regard to economy, by which the aged, orderly, and infirm, are sometimes deprived of a part of their comfort, or the charge on the contributor is of necessity increased; so that what is given to the undeserving may be considered a species of robbery on the really distressed indigent. I would therefore have all beggars, except in some peculiar instances, as well as all idle and disorderly persons who live by devices injurious to the morals of the public, sent into his Majesty's service, or to our colonies abroad, if able men; the luxuries, in many instances, enjoyed by beggars, being an insult on the hard-working man, by holding him out as a dupe who toils to earn a living much inferior to what is got by canting and deception.

It has been stated by Mr. Colquhoun, as an argument against workhouses, or more properly speaking, poor-houses, according to the plan on which they are at present conducted, that in 1803 there were 957,248 persons relieved out of houses, at an expense of $3l. 3s. 7\frac{1}{4}d.$ per head per annum, whereas 83,468 were maintained in houses at an expense of $12l. 3s. 6\frac{3}{4}d.$ per head per annum. At first sight this may appear a good objection to the keeping of poor in houses; but I apprehend the opinion will be changed, when it is taken into consideration that the latter number were *permanently* relieved in a great number of houses, without suitable employment; for their earnings are only calculated at $3s. 9d.$ per head per annum; whereas had they been congregated into fewer houses, as I shall propose, and been employed in some profitable way, the expense would have been much reduced by a cheaper mode of living, in consequence of numbers and better management, as also by considerable

additional earnings ; or it may reasonably
be presumed that the above-stated 83,468
are part of the 166,000 of really impotent,
as stated in p. 18. If so, that may account
for the additional proportionate expense :
whereas about one-third part of the former
number were only *partially* relieved; for
out of 1,040,716 who received relief in 1803,
there were 305,899 who received only *occasional* relief; and also 194,052 vagrants,
whose relief was only temporary, having cost
but 2*s.* per head per annum, as will be seen
by referring to p. 14 ; and amongst those
who received permanent relief were 315,150
children, the expense of whose keep cannot
be equal to adults. With a view of further
proving the efficacy of my intended proposal,
I will state the advantages arising from
similar local institutions, beginning with that
of the Isle of Wight, which was established
a few years ago, and where they borrowed a
large sum of money to erect a building, and
put the poor to work in one house, by which
they reduced the expense of the poor from
s. 3*d.* per head per week to 2*s.*, besides
paying the interest of the sum borrowed, and
also discharging part of the principal annually.

Christ-Church and Spitalfields workhouses

D

in London are on the plan of setting the paupers to work, who have earned 950l. a year, although they consisted principally of children and aged persons, to the number of about 330. I will mention further the savings in other well regulated houses of industry, to show the practicability, as well as utility, even were the regulations I shall mention confined to *local situations only*. At Shrewsbury, for instance, they reduced the expense after opening the house of *industry*, 16,000l. At Balcamp, in Suffolk, a debt of 12,000l. was paid off, and 1,000l. remained in hand for future contingencies. At Somer a debt of 8,000l. was reduced to 180l.

These several advantages have arisen by setting the poor to work, and good management ; and if such savings are practicable in these instances, it is reasonable to suppose that immense sums might be saved to the public by a general adoption ; for at present, I believe, out of 14,318 parishes there are only 774 who maintain their poor by special Acts, viz. 215 in Norfolk, 253 in Suffolk, 32 in Middlesex, 259 in 21 other counties, and 15 in Wales. Some persons may be of opinion that by equalizing the rates the property in certain places would be diminished in value, under the idea of an augmentation of the

rates in those places. If this should happen
at all, it would only be in a very small degree
and limited extent; for by returns made to
Parliament up to the year 1803, it appears
that the whole average of rates was 4s. 5¼d.
including county rates, &c. which amounted
to a trifle under 10d. in the pound, which re-
duces the sum paid for the maintenance of the
poor to 3s. 7¼d. per pound on the sum of
24,129,134l. being the rental on which the
poor rates were collected in 1803; and I will
suppose a saving of 1s. per pound only, on
the average, by the proposed regulations,
which would on the above sum amount to
1,206,456l.; and it would reduce the amount
of the average, as in 1803, to 2s. 7¼d.; and
there were in the same year only two counties, and part of Yorkshire, where the rates
averaged less, viz. Northumberland, which
were 1s. 8¾d.; Durham, 2s. 4¼d.; North of
Yorkshire, 2s. 6¾d.; East of Yorkshire, 2s.
7¾d.; which included the county rates, and
will reduce the above as a charge on the poor,
as much as the county rates were. The rates
for Gloucestershire and Rutlandshire were so
near the supposed reduced average, after de-
ducting 10d. for county rates, &c. (if they
amounted to so much) that the difference is
not worth notice, being only one farthing

each. It therefore appears that few places, taking the average of counties as an example, would be injured, whilst so many would be benefited; and some particular parishes are so heavily burthened as to make the property of but little value; and the poor in those places exhibit a most miserable appearance : so upon the whole it may be fairly presumed that the advantages arising to a great majority, if not to the whole community, would more than counterbalance a small addition to the most favoured places.

Having stated thus much on the efficacy of the proposed alteration, I will proceed, secondly, to give the outlines of the general plan for adoption.

First, then, I would recommend a repeal of all the obnoxious existing laws, and in lieu thereof an Act of Parliament (for without compulsion the best plans are seldom efficacious) for the sale or disposal of all houses, lands, &c. which are at present appropriated or used as poor-houses or workhouses, provided they are exclusively the property of the respective parishes, excepting such as may be calculated as useful for the present proposed undertaking, and apply the produce towards purchasing land, and erecting other suitable buildings, in districts not exceeding 15 or 20 miles from the centre, choosing such situations as are the most likely to afford employment, and other needful conveniences, on such a plan as to be capable of furnishing employment, and oblige such as are able, to earn their own living, as far as their strength and ability will allow them, to prevent dissipation and vice, and to provide a comfortable abode for the aged and infirm when unable to work, and be the means of training up the infant poor, to habits of industry, religion, and virtue, and making them useful members of society; which houses should receive, *first*, children whose parents are unable to support them; *second*, adults capable of work, but who have not the means of procuring it; *third*, the really impotent. For the first and second description, the requisite materials should be provided to set them on work, and have the children educated, and in proper time put out apprentices; and for the third, an habitation and necessary relief afforded.

The system on which workhouses are at present generally conducted, and the poor provided for, operates as an encouragement to idleness; for there is seldom but little compulsion to profitable labour, and in many instances none at all. Some persons who have wrote against workhouses are of opinion that they operate against the general industry of the labouring poor, by giving them a dependance on something else. Perhaps in the way they are now mostly conducted, it may; but if all are required and compelled to work who are admitted, and able, and no relief given without it, excepting to the very young, aged, and infirm, it surely must act as a stimulus to all to endeavour to get their own living, if possible, without application for relief, knowing that they will be compelled to work, if able, and in some measure be deprived of liberty. Nor can it be considered unreasonable to require persons to work; for by the laws of both God and nature all persons who have strength and ability are required to labour for their own subsistence, and not be burthensome to the community. So far from this acting hard upon them, it is rather adding to their happiness; for idleness excites the most dangerous fermentation of the passions, and produces in the mind of the idle a crowd of ideas and irregular desires inimical to their happiness, or to that of the public; for persons who are indolent and slothful must inevitably become melancholy and miserable; they can never do any good, nor apply themselves to any thing useful: if

the present offers nothing, they will be look-
ing back on the past, which may in all probability afford them but a dismal and dreary
prospect. Besides, idleness is the soil which
all kind of vice thrives the best in; it therefore ought not to be cultivated, for it leads to
profligacy, and that to disease and poverty
irremediable.

Secondly: The Act might also empower the
Trustees, consisting of a Governor and Directors to each district, to borrow money for
the purpose of purchasing land for building,
or for any other purpose connected with the
government of the poor, and to allow a sum
of money to be raised yearly, in addition to
what is required to maintain the poor, equal
to one-twentieth part of the sum borrowed,
to be laid out to accumulate with compound
interest, which will enable the whole to be
paid off in fifteen years, when both principal
and interest will cease; and at that time a
much greater benefit will be experienced by
the contributors.

Thirdly: When each district is fixed, a
return then to be made of the average
number of poor in every parish in each proposed division for the three previous years, to
ascertain nearly the size of the house required, and also the necessary quantity of

land, which should be an acre for every forty persons, for a garden. This is an essential thing; as vegetables will save considerably the consumption of meat, and form a cheaper and equally salutary food; and the refuse of the garden would assist in keeping pigs for the use of the house; and if a suitable quantity of land could be had for keeping cows, it would add much to the comfort of the poor, and be a great saving.

Fourthly: In every county or district, or perhaps in every other one, where they are small, there should be a house for the purpose of receiving the abandoned and vile, so as to keep them as much as possible from the worthy aged, disabled, and unfortunate; and they should be employed on work of the worst kind, and their supply of food be according to their respective deserts; which would operate as a punishment, and be the means probably of working in them some reformation, and also prevent that communication between the good and the bad, which might prove injurious to the former; and certainly a difference should be made between the really unfortunate and the abandoned, wicked, and idle, as much as there should be different punishments for different species of crimes. Fear of want and severe punishment are perhaps the most effectual discouragers of vice; hence, those persons, also, who add to the stock of paupers by illegitimate children, should receive some kind of deprivation in order to discourage a vice so flagitious.

Fifthly: A valuation to be made of all lands, houses, and other ratable property in each district, and a sum to be collected sufficient to answer the demand: at the end of each year an account to be sent to the office in London, to be called the " *National Poor Office*," which, when compared with the whole valuation and collection, if it is more in any division than its equitable proportion, it must be reimbursed from the general fund; if it is less, then to be charged with the deficiency the following year.

Sixthly: All new erected houses, or such as are capable of alteration, should be built in a *plain* and *economical* manner, representing the objects they are intended to give shelter to, more than that national grandeur which is too often aimed at in erecting houses for charitable uses; which houses should contain one room large enough to dine in, &c.; and each bed-room to hold six beds and twelve persons, with recesses in the bed-rooms of about 18 inches to take the heads of the beds, this will save the use of curtains, which are both expensive and dangerous. The receptacles for the beds to be of cast-iron, which are to be had at Colebrook-dale at about 30s. each; they have holes in the bottom like a cullender, and those with iron feet are the best; they are not only cheap and durable, but also a preventive against vermin. The houses to be well ventilated, and washed with quick-lime once a-year, which will destroy insects, and add to the health and comfort of the occupiers; for dwellings suffered to become foul generate malignant diseases, and weaken the springs of life. There should be also a room for the sick, work-rooms, &c.

Seventhly: To each house appoint (according to the population) a Governor, Directors, Guardians, besides Overseers; the Overseers to collect the rates and pay the same immediately into the hands of the Treasurer of the district, who should be appointed by the Directors and Guardians. The Guardians and Overseers to be chosen annually at vestry-meetings, or at a general meeting of every parish to be held yearly on a specified day. The Directors to be chosen by ballot out of the Guardians, and the Governors from the Directors. The Directors and Guardians to hold meetings every three months, with fines for non-attendance,—say one to five

pounds. The Directors and Guardians chosen and refusing to serve, to fine,—say twenty
pounds for Directors, and fifteen pounds for
Guardians: all fines to go in aid of the rates.
It must appear obvious that Directors and
Guardians should be compelled to act, or fine
largely, and that one fine should only excuse
them one year, and that they should be persons of some consideration in life ; for it is
well known that without compulsion, persons
will seldom continue to do their duty ; for
what they at first attend to through novelty
or ambition, they in a short time give up for
want of some interested view or other stimulus.
A proportionate number of Directors and
Guardians to act monthly in rotation, or fine
five pounds for non-attendance, unless prevented by illness or some other cause satis-
factory to the Directors and Guardians at the
quarterly meeting. Qualifications for Directors and Guardians, sixty pounds a year, real
or funded property, or one hundred and
twenty pounds rental. One Director, Guar-
dian, or Overseer, to visit the house in rotation once a week, or once a fortnight if the
distance exceeds six miles, to inspect every
part of the premises, the stores, provisions,
&c. and report the state of them ; and how
many persons are in the house, number out

of work, and the cause, which enter in a book with remarks, ideas of improvement, or any mismanagement, to be produced and considered on at every quarterly meeting.

Eighthly: A Treasurer to be appointed by the Directors and Guardians, on whom orders are to be given by four Directors or Guardians for the payment of money; he (the Treasurer) to give security if required.

Ninthly: A Master and Mistress to be appointed by the Directors, &c. to whom allow in lieu of salary, or in part of it, a certain profit on the nett earnings, which will make them more diligent to procure work, as they will have an interest as well as a duty to perform; and they must be required to keep a book for the purpose of entering any complaint or improper conduct of any inmate, for the inspection of the Guardians, &c.

Tenthly: When any persons are admitted into the house, they should be examined regarding the fitness of continuing their own apparel, and also as to their state of body, that no infectious disorder may be introduced; the master should likewise take an account of what trade or employment they have been accustomed to, which will be the means of employing them to greater advantage.

Eleventhly: A Schoolmaster and Mistress

to be appointed from amongst the poor, if any are competent, to instruct the children who are too young for work, daily, on Dr. Bell's plan of education, with improvements, if practicable ; and those who are capable of work to be instructed one hour in each day alternately, so as not to have too many from their work at one time, and the best scholars to read a chapter in turn every Sunday evening to the rest, or to a select number, so that each may distinctly hear ; also distribute occasional rewards, which will stir up emulation in them : by this and suitable correction for faults and inculcating habits of industry, they will be made fit to go into the world when at a proper age, and be able to maintain themselves, it is to be hoped, without further assistance. May we not expect by so doing to prevent the corruption of vice and its natural companions, poverty and disease, and create a reformation in the morals of the rising generation by such treatment, in addition to the observance of what has been already recommended ; and furthermore, to instil into the minds of the young, piety to God, benevolence to men, justice, charity, temperance and sobriety, in preference to allowing them to run about the streets in rags and nastiness, associating with their fellows in

2

iniquity, and imbibing every thing that is bad; for it is well known the human character is soon debased by association with the wicked.

Twelfthly: All who are in the house in health and capable, should be required to attend divine service twice every Sunday, and those whose health will not allow of such attendance, to be read to by the Master, Mistress, Schoolmaster, or some other fit person ; for there is no doubt but ninety out of one hundred become poor through the contempt of religion, and the abuse of the good things of this life.

Thirteenthly : Appoint rewards or superior indulgences to the orderly and industrious, and punishment for the lazy, filthy, or those who talk obscenely, or swear.

Fourteenthly: Neither the Master, Mistress, or any other person but those appointed by the Directors and Guardians, to be allowed to sell any thing made or manufactured in the house; nor allow any wines, liquors, or ale, to be brought into the house or premises, unless ordered by the medical attendant.

Fifteenthly : Persons requiring relief, to be recommended by the Directors or Guardians, (if any) Clergyman, or Overseers of the parish they are in, they being more competent to judge of the wants of individuals or families who reside near them than any others.

Sixteenthly : No single persons or married ones without families to be relieved out of the house by any pension, because considerably less will keep them in the house than out, they being in general bad managers ; excepting persons requiring temporary immediate relief; in those instances the Overseers, Guardians, or Directors, to order the same for one week.

Seventeenthly : Those with families who require relief out of the house should be visited by one of the Overseers to prevent imposition, or be allowed to send part of their family to the workhouse in proportion to the relief required.

It may be proper to remark on this proposition, in answer to Sir F. Eden, who has said that " Houses of Industry remove the young from their parents, and destroy that domestic social connexion which should subsist between parents and children," that the same reasoning would apply also with respect to parents putting their children apprentices, to servitude, or any other employment from home: if parents are unable to maintain their own offspring, they should surely be thankful that a provision is made for them by others, when there is no other alternative than that, or seeing them in a state of want and misery; besides, do not the middle classes of society, and also the opulent, send their children from home, and sometimes to distant parts, where there is but a poor chance of ever seeing them again?.

Eighteenthly: The Guardians to see to putting out the children to trades or employ-ment when at a suitable age.

Nineteenthly: All persons who are capable of work to be employed every day, Sundays, Christmas Day, and Good Friday, excepted; for so many hours as the day light in the dif-ferent seasons will allow, not exceeding ten or twelve hours, or less, according to the age and strength of the parties, allowing them half an hour to breakfast, one hour to dinner, and half an hour to supper; a bell to be rung when they go to meals, and return to work.

Twentiethly: Every one to wash their hands before they eat their meals, and to put on a clean shirt or shift every Sunday morn-ing, and the men to be shaved at least once a week.

Twenty-firstly: The beds or mattresses to be put in order every day, and the rooms swept and dusted twice a week by young girls in the house, who should be alternately employed in household work to prepare them for servitude.

Twenty-secondly : Two men or two women, or a man and wife, to occupy one bed, and to be so paired, that if one is deprived of sight or any other faculty, he should associate with another who is possessed of that faculty, in order to render him assistance.

Twenty-thirdly : Males and females to be kept separate, as far as the nature of employment will allow.

Twenty-fourthly : If any person shall refuse to obey the just commands of the Master or Mistress, or be guilty of swearing, indecent behaviour, or any immoral action, or be quarrelsome, he shall receive some suitable punishment.

Twenty-fifthly : If any persons shall wilfully waste or spoil any goods or work under their care, or on which they are employed, they are to be punished for so doing.

Twenty-sixthly and lastly : The rules and regulations to be printed large, and hung up in the house and work-rooms, and read out at least once a month, or oftener, if any fresh person is admitted.

E

EMPLOYMENT.

The work on which the poor are to be employed must depend on the situation in which each house is placed ; some articles and work are in greater demand in one place than another. Such persons as have been brought up to trades, viz. taylors, shoemakers, blacksmiths, carpenters, weavers, &c. to be employed in their respective trades : a forge should be in some part of the premises where the smiths might fill up their time in making nails and other articles for sale. A number might also be employed in pin making, in drawing the wire, polishing, cutting into lengths, pointing, head making, putting on the heads, papering, &c. &c. : others in picking oakum, spinning twine, carding and spinning wool, making baskets, hassocks, sacks, &c. beating, hackling, and spinning hemp. The women and girls in some places spin it by a wheel, so contrived as to draw a thread with each hand ; by which method two can earn equal to three with one hand only. Old women, girls, and little boys, may spin thread and yarn ; also knit yarn stockings and gloves. It is known that most old women can spin, even if their eye-sight is bad ; for

it is by the touch more than sight they do it;
others may sew, so that every thing they
wear may be made in the house, besides what
may be sold and afford profit ; and moderate
employment, as I have already observed, will
add much to their comfort and happiness,
requiring no more from the aged and orderly
than their strength will allow ; nor can it be
objected to under a supposition that it will
interfere with the independent workman, so
long as there is an increasing demand for
labour; because none can be thrown out of
employ, consequently none can be injured,
unless it may be called so by such persons
trying to make an unfair profit by keeping the
supply below the demand ; and that being an
act of injustice, it cannot appear on due consideration that, by securing employment for
the poor in workhouses, any danger can arise
to any other part of the community. The
garden ground should of course be cultivated
by the poor in the house, and care should be
taken to keep it free from weeds, which impoverish and injure the land : especial care
should also be taken to keep it well stocked
with potatoes, cabbages, spinach, carrots,
parsnips, turnips, peas, beans, herbs, and
onions; for great savings are to be made by

increasing the consumption of vegetables. " Onions," says Sir John Sinclair, (and which opinion I confirm from my own knowledge) " cannot be sufficiently recommended ; they possess more nourishment than perhaps any other vegetable. It is a well known fact, that a Highlander with a few raw onions in his pocket, and a crust of bread or a bit of cake, can work or travel to an almost incredible extent for two or three days together without any other sort of food whatever. Onions agree particularly with persons of a cold phlegmatic habit, when the stomach is weak and relaxed; and where it requires the aid of a powerful stimulus to assist digestion ; " they also act as a soporific, and consequently are of great use to such persons as are deprived of sleep.

I should recommend the whole consumption of the house to be produced on the premises, as far as is possible ; and oxen, sheep, &c. to be purchased at first hand, and slaughtered for the house, disposing of such as is not wanted, by which it has been proved great savings have been made where similar methods have been adopted.

Let out the poor to persons in the neighbourhood wanting any assistance for gardening, working on the roads, going on errands, weeding, washing, ironing, or any other work, on reasonable terms.

Also keep a register of all persons or children in the house capable of work, for the inspection of such as are in want of servants and apprentices.

The following is suggested as proper diet.

For Breakfast.—Milk pottage. Barley broth. Rice milk. Bread and cheese occasionally: also gruel or burgou, which is something thicker than gruel. It may be boiled in large coppers, and not made so thick as hasty pudding. It is eaten with molasses; and the expense about three half-pence a meal.

For Dinner.—Butcher's meat, with plenty of vegetables. Ox cheeks and shins of beef stewed, with vegetables. Pork stewed, with peas-pudding. Rice puddings boiled, or dumplings: one pound for grown persons: half to three quarters of a pound for children is considered sufficient. Bread and cheese, with onions, once a week. Meat broth made as follows has been found to be cheap and good, viz.: 3 lb. meat, 2 lb. barley, 10 lb. potatoes, 4 lb. bread, 40 lb. water, is together 59 lb., to be boiled away to 48 lb., which will be sufficient for 32 persons, allowing

$1\frac{1}{4}$ lb. to each. A few onions or leeks boiled with it will much improve it. The expense for each person per meal will be about five farthings to three half-pence.

Again, peas broth made as follows is also a good and a cheap article of food : 4 lb. peas, $2\frac{1}{2}$ lb. barley, 10 lb. potatoes, 4 lb. bread, 40 lb. water, with onions or leeks, is $60\frac{1}{4}$ lb., boiled until reduced to 48 lb., is $1\frac{1}{4}$ lb. each for 32 persons.

Count Rumford, who has paid much attention to cookery, has given the following receipt : a tea-cup full of pearl barley, and one gallon of water, boil gently for half an hour; then add 3 lb. of lean beef or neck of mutton, some carrots and turnips cut small, a pint of green peas, if to be got, and some onions : let the whole boil gently for two hours longer, in a close soup kettle, when the broth will be fit for use.

The following receipts have been given to me as worthy of notice :—

I. Four lb. salt pork or beef cut small, put into a pot with 12 quarts of water; boil it slow for three quarters of an hour; then put in a few parsnips, carrots, or turnips, cut small, or a few sliced potatoes and cabbages; thicken it with oatmeal, and season with salt and pepper.

II. Two lb. beef, mutton, or pork, cut into small pieces, a quart of peas, 16 turnips sliced, two dozen potatoes cut very small, 8 onions, to all of which put 14 quarts of water; let the whole boil gently over a slow fire two hours and a half; thicken it with 1 lb of oatmeal; after it is put in, boil it a quarter of an hour longer, stirring it all the time, and season it with pepper and salt.

III. Four lb. beef, 6 to 8 onions, 20 turnips, 1 lb. rice, a couple of handfuls parsley, thyme, and savory, some pepper and salt, 16 quarts of water; the beef to be cut in slices, and when it has boiled some time, cut it still smaller; let the whole boil moderately for two hours, or it may be stewed in an oven and warmed up as wanted; oatmeal and potatoes may be added to thicken it.

To make Ox Cheek Soup.—To one cheek put two pecks of potatoes, a quarter of a peck of onions, an ounce of black pepper, half a pound of salt, boiled altogether in 45 quarts of water till reduced to 30, and to which may be added any kind of vegetables; a pint of this soup with a bit of the meat warmed up, is a dinner for a grown person.

For Supper.—Potatoes two or three times a week, which may be varied in dressing, so as to make them more palatable. Mashed

potatoes from ¾ lb. to 1¼ lb. for grown persons, and 8 to 10 oz. for children, will prove
an excellent substitute for bread and cheese
in dear times. It has been ascertained, by
returns made to Parliament, that the paupers
in counties where potatoes are in general use
are fewer in proportion than where they are
not: and the great increase in the population
of Ireland, which is more than four times
what it was 110 years ago, where they live
principally on that root, is a proof of its
nutritive quality. Broth or stew left at
dinner might be occasionally allowed: also
bread and cheese, with or without onions,
and sometimes part of a red herring to each.

Rice is most excellent food, and furnishes
subsistence to perhaps more human beings
than all other grains put together: it sits easy
on the stomach, and is fit for invalids.

N. B. The sick to have fresh meat, broth,
&c., as may be thought necessary by the
medical attendant.

Bread may be made much cheaper, I am
informed, than is generally done, and equally
nutritious, by taking out of the flour only
the coarse flake bran; of which take 10 lb.,
or any proportionate quantity, which boil in
eight gallons of water: when smooth it will
produce 7¼ gallons of clear bran water: with

it knead 112 lb. flour, putting to it salt and yeast, as is usual; divide it into loaves, and bake it. By this method there will be one-fifth more of bread than usual, because this quantity of flour will take six quarts more of bran water than of plain. This bread is said to be preferable for weak stomachs: but that made of wheat and rye mixed is the best for the generality. Wheat alone, being of a starchy nature, is apt to occasion constipation: and all rye is too slippery for the bowels.

I refer farther to Edlin's treatise on bread, making one volume octavo, 1805, in which are receipts for making peas bread, &c. for the labouring poor.

The following bill of fare is taken from the Isle of Wight workhouse, which I have referred to in the former part of this work.

	Breakfast.	Dinner.	Supper.
Sunday....	Bread and cheese.	Mutton, beef, or pork, dumpling, or pudding.	Broth.
Monday ..	Broth.	Baked suet pudding.	Bread and cheese.
Tuesday ..	Bread and cheese.	Rice milk.	Ditto.
Wednesday	Ditto.	Same as Sunday.	Broth.
Thursday..	Broth.	Baked rice pudding.	Bread and cheese.
Friday	Bread and cheese.	Same as Sunday.	Ditto.
Saturday ..	Ditto.	Broth thickened with rice.	Ditto.

Clothing.

The refuse of flax, which is called backings of tow, would make comfortable clothing of the fustian or cotton kind, which I should think might be purchased at a quarter of the expense of wool. Women and children might spin it, weavers make it, and then have it dyed.

All the poor should have some mark of distinction to detect them when out of the house, if found begging, or guilty of any other fault.

Drink.

I have not made any remark on what is proper drink: that I should rather leave to the judgment of the managers, or to that of medical men. The use of liquid food is, I understand, intended to dilute the solid, and to preserve the blood in a proper state of fluidity. It is thought that if $1\frac{1}{4}$ lb. of solid food is taken in 24 hours, then it is proper to take 3 lb. of liquid, which is about three pints. What the quality should be, I do not mean to determine. I have known old people take a good draught of water the last thing going to bed, and first in the morning, who found great comfort from it. Indeed, I can speak experimentally of its good effect on weak stomachs; and I also remember having heard it said that a Gentleman was advised to try a chalybeate spring, which he did; and after he left it he drank from his own pump every morning a rummer of cold water, and found equal benefit, which induced him to put on his pump the following distich:—

"O! steel, thou art a cheat,
It's the water does the feat."

After this remark, it may be as well to give the opinion of Hoffman, who was a most respectable medical author; he says, " Water is the fittest drink for all persons of all ages and temperaments; of all the productions of nature or art it comes the nearest to that universal remedy so much searched after by mankind, but never discovered. By its fluidity and mildness, it promotes a free and equable circulation of the blood and humours through all the vessels of the body, upon which the due performance of every animal function depends; and hence water drinkers are not only the most active and nimble, but also the most cheerful and sprightly of all people.

" In sanguine complexions, water, by diluting the blood, renders the circulation easy and uniform. In the choleric, the coolness of the water restrains the quick motion and intense heat of the humours. It attenuates the glutinous viscidity of the juices of the phlegmatic, and the gross earthiness which prevails in melancholic temperaments. And as to different ages, water is good for children to make their tenacious milky diet thin and easy to digest; for youth and middle aged, to sweeten and dissolve any scorbutic acrimony or sharpness that may be in the humours, by which means pains and obstructions are prevented; and for old people, to moisten and mollify their rigid fibres, and to promote a less difficult circulation through their hard and shrivelled vessels."

All animals except man reject every liquor but water.

If what is spent in purchasing strong liquors was appropriated to buying nourishing food, and other necessaries of life, mankind would live longer, be more healthy, stronger, and happier, than they now are. This doctrine cannot be too strongly nor too frequently mentioned and enforced.

The following method I beg to recommend for keeping the weekly account, to show each week's consumption of provisions, and the number of persons in the house.

Quality of Provisions.	Left last week.		Bought this week.		Total received.		Left this week.		Expended.		Price.		Total of Cost.		
	st.	lb.	st.	lb.	st.	lb.	st.	lb.	st.	lb.	s.	d.	l.	s.	d.
Beef	20	0	22	10	42	10	19	0	23	10	7	6	8	17	6
Ox cheeks and shins	.....		....		....		.....		.....		....		2	12	6
Mutton	1	6	2	4	3	10	1	4	2	6	7	0	0	17	0
Pork	5	0	2	1	7	1	5	1	2	0	7	0	0	14	0
Butter	......		0	6	0	6	0	1	0	5	1	2	0	5	10
Cheese	50	0	....		50	0	14	0	6	0	3	0	2	8	0
Bread	58	0	30	0	88	0	40	0	48	0	3	0	7	4	0
Peas	20 bu.		11 bu.		31 bu.		20 bu.		11 bu.		13	0	7	3	0
Potatoes	80	0	....		80	0	16	0	64	0	2	1	6	13	4
Candles	0	5	0	3	0	8	0	2	0	6	1	1	0	6	6
Soap	......		0	13	0	13	0	7	0	6	0	10	0	5	0
Salt	0	8	0	7	0	15	0	11	0	4	0	3	0	1	0
Treacle	3	0	2	0	5	0	2	7	2	7	7	0	0	17	6
Flour	1	0	....		1	0	0	6	0	8	3	1	0	1	10
Oatmeal	2 bu.		....		2 bu.		1½ bu.		½ bu.		11	6	0	5	9
Beer	72 gal.		36 gal.		108 gal.		80 gal.		28 gal.		0	8	0	18	8
Milk	......		50 gal.		50 gal.		......		50 gal.		0	8	1	13	4
Groceries	.....		....		....		.....		.....		....		2	1	0
Rice	14	0	10	0	24	0	6	0	18	0	5	0	4	10	0
Red herrings	......		....		....		.....		.....		....		2	0	0
White ditto	......		....		....		.....		.....		....		1	4	0
													50	19	9

340 persons in the house, including 58 children at 3s... ....51 0 0

THE END.